College for Me:

A College Guide for Students with Attention Deficit Disorder

Christina L. Bryce

Illustrations by: Michelle Amerine

ISBN: 1-4116-5815-9
Illustrations by: Michelle Amerine

Contents

Acknowledgments

I would like to take the time to thank my parents for defending my need for services since the first day I required them. Without my parents, I would not be where I am today.

I would like to recognize and thank the following individuals at Rochester Institute of Technology for making this book possible: Dr. Stanley McKenzie, Provost and VP for Academic Affairs; Dr. Mary-Beth Cooper, VP for Student Affairs; and Dr. James Myers, Director, Center for Multidisciplinary Studies.

I would also like to thank RIT's ASC (Academic Support Center), TRiO, faculty, and staff for their outstanding services for students with disabilities. Without the services and helpful faculty members, many of us students could be lost.

Many thanks to Tim Laemmermann, Mark Greenberg, and Shannon Baker for allowing me to share their experiences with Attention Deficit Disorder and their learning disabilities. With special thanks to my two editors, Mary Bonaparte-Krogh and Marianne Buehler. Without their assistance, this book would not be possible. To my designer, Michelle Amerine, you did an excellent job with all of the images in this book. Thank you.

To my fiancé, Kevin Hui, thank you for all of your help with my college homework and for bearing with me while writing this book.

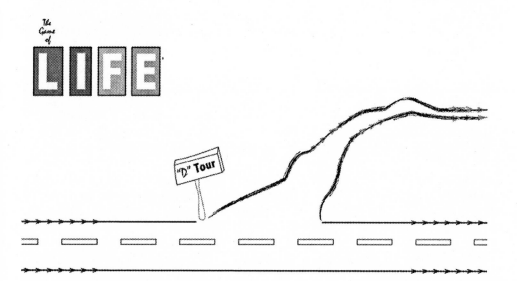

Preface

A high school graduation is supposed to be one of the happiest days of your life. That day can be dismal if you are watching your friends going to universities and colleges and at the same time, the high school guidance counselor, high school teachers, parents, and friends are telling you, "You are not capable of succeeding in college." For some students, college may not be the right choice, but for people who are determined to succeed and who are motivated to learn, this book will help you make the transition successfully from high school to college.

This is the true story of my experience as a college student with Attention Deficit Disorder (ADD). The book is not written by a medical doctor or a psychologist; it is written by a regular person with ADD who has accomplished what many people have said was impossible. I found it helpful to hear advice and feedback from students who are in college with a learning disability, rather than hearing it from the doctors and professionals who have not experienced the challenges.

In today's world, education is essential. In order to have the career that you desire, you must gain the required skills and have a college background. For students with a learning disability, searching for a university can be very difficult. In many respects, a high school environment is very different from a college-level environment.

To make the most of your education, it is important to know what your learning style is (see Chapter 3) and that you seek the appropriate assistance when you need it. This book will help you find the information services that you may need.

Are you thinking, "Where do I fit in? Can I make it in a university?" Hopefully, by the time you finish this book, you will have the confidence needed to succeed in college and have the satisfying life you want and deserve.

Chapter 1: My Story

My name is Christina Bryce. I was born in California and was adopted by my Aunt and Uncle at two years old. We then moved to Pennsylvania. When I started kindergarten, my teacher noticed that I had a difficult time learning new things and remembering. I was sent to a number of doctors to find out why. After the tests were completed, it was determined by a BEAM study (a test to map a person's brain activity) that I had a right mid-temporal dysfunction and neuropathy, in other words, ADD. I repeated kindergarten because I was behind in skills and language. In 1st grade through 12th grade, I was placed in study skills and special education classes. In these classes, I received individual attention from teachers in a one-on-one environment. It was a small classroom (about 5-8 students in one classroom) with students who had ADD and other learning disabilities like me. I also received accommodations, which are services that help me learn better, such as, untimed tests, phonetic spelling, and teacher notes for all class subjects. By using the teacher notes for classes, I could pay more attention to what was being said in class. The notes also contained the correct spelling and were clearer to read than my own handwriting.

I did not think anything was "wrong" with me until 4th grade, when I was placed in a regular classroom for the first part of the day, and then sent to my special education class for the remainder of the day. I often had teachers fetch me from my regular classroom for speech therapy class or my math class.

When the other students saw that I was leaving the regular class, I would often hear, "Where is she going? Why can't we go with her?" These comments made me start to realize that I was "different."

Being in school became more miserable as I moved through the grades each year. In a public school, students with learning disabilities are offered only limited support. By the time I entered 7th grade, I had a 2nd grade math level, 5th grade reading level, and I had a very difficult time trying to spell any word. I was placed into special ed classes again.

During Middle School, I left school for health reasons. I had two spinal fusions for scoliosis. It was a painful surgery that included the installation of 4 titanium bars and 27 hooks in my back.

After missing school for a year for surgery and recovery, I returned to school and entered Council Rock High School in Newtown, PA. This was when I decided to start taking responsibility for my education by attending my Individual Education Plan (IEP) meetings. For ten years, my teachers, parents, the principal, and the Director of Education had held meetings to plan my education—without me. I finally realized that this was *my* education and I wanted to make sure that I would be able to take the classes that interested me in addition to the classes that were required.

I gathered all the necessary information that everyone involved needed to have in order to plan the year's education for me. I thought about entering a technical school in my community. As an alternative to high school, technical schools teach hands-on career skills to high school-age students. I studied Developmental Child Care for a half day and then took a school bus back to my high school for my special ed classes. This worked out well, because I was taking a class that I was interested in and fulfilling my degree requirements at the same time. My parents were concerned that I would not be able to handle the regular workload at the tech school because they did not have services for learning-disabled students. I was not worried about the lack of services at the tech school, because I wanted to see if I could make it in school without my usual services. Once I was there and realized how different the workload was from my special ed class, I asked my teachers for help.

The teacher contacted my high school to have my records sent over. I began to receive some support. I did not get as much help as my high school gave me, but it made a big difference.

By the time I entered 12th grade, my learning levels had gone up a bit. I was doing better in reading, with a 6th grade reading level. My math was still the same. In my senior year, I had done very well in my childcare tech school classes, especially after they started to accommodate my learning styles. My parents were thrilled that I was able to advocate for myself.

In my senior year, the public school created a new special ed program; they called it "contained learning." To save money, they had eliminated the special ed classes that I was accustomed to by trying to mainstream as many students as possible. With this policy, the school took the students whose tests scores were below a certain level and placed them all in one classroom. The high school did not know where to place me in the academic environment.

Most of the students in my class had been in classes with me throughout my school years. At the beginning of the year, we were taught very basic elementary skills, but I noticed by the middle of the year, we were still going over the same material we had done at the beginning of the year.

I began to get bored with my classes and asked my mom if there was a more challenging special ed class I could take. However, the contained learning was all the public school could offer me. If I was to enroll in regular classes, I would be too far behind and the pace would be too fast. I could not afford to go to a private school. I was in the middle of the learning curve and was stuck in a very basic-skills class. Towards the end of high school, I began to consider college; at least I would be challenged.

I had a part-time job at a local supermarket, but to me, it was just an after-school job. At first, when I told my parents that I wanted to go to college, they were glad but concerned at the same time. My mom thought it would be a good idea to stay at the supermarket for a few years to see how the job progressed. She said they had very good benefits there. My mom did not intend to discourage me, but I felt dispirited.

I knew I was fully capable of going to college. I did not want to work at a supermarket for the rest of my life. I turned to my high school guidance counselor for answers. She opened the big, messy folder that held all my academic information. Any ADD student who has studied through twelve years of school knows about the never-ending flow of paperwork that is involved in having ADD. She looked at my IQ tests, grades and scores. According to my test scores, I could never make it into a university and it was not worth trying. Again, my spirit was crushed, but it did not stop me.

I decided to go forward and apply to colleges on my own without asking for advice or comments from anyone. I applied at the local community college to get started and to get a feel for the environment. I was accepted and started classes in the Fall. I also received a full academic scholarship to the local community college for excelling in my childcare classes.

While attending the community college, I searched for and was admitted to a four-year university. The details of my experience applying to and finishing my education form the chapters of this book. With all of the difficulties I have had in my education and life, going to college has brought out the best in me and confirmed what I am capable of.

I have proven to everyone who doubted me that I have the same chance to succeed as anyone else.

Currently, at Rochester Institute of Technology (RIT), I have a 3.8 GPA and I am on the Dean's List. I have earned an Associate's Degree with High Honors. I am completing my Bachelor's Degree and two certificates at RIT. I plan to graduate from RIT in February 2006. After I graduate and I am working in the printing industry, my goal is to work my way up to a management position for an on-demand printing company. Looking back on my college life, I am grateful I had the chance to succeed. I have been through many challenges in my life and have seen and learned many new things. Also, I have done most of it on my own. I will always remember the many people who have helped me in my academic and personal life.

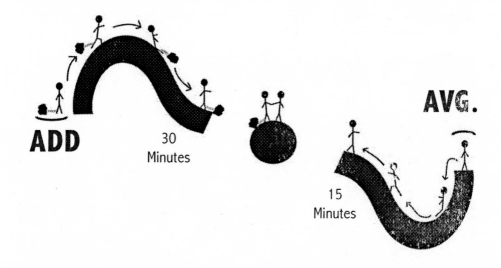

Chapter 2: What is ADD?

Definitions of Attention Deficit Disorder can be written in a very complex way with many technical medical terms which are sometimes difficult to understand. Here is an example:

"Attention Deficit Disorder is a dysfunction of the central nervous system, most specifically the reticular activation system, which results in difficulties of maintaining attention and concentration, learning and memory, as well as involving an inability to process and sort out incoming information or stimulus from both an individual's inner (subjective) and outer (objective) worlds." (Natural Pure Health 1999)

You may be wondering, "What does this mean?" This paraphrase explains the definition: 'We' have problems with our short-term memory. Here's an example: My mom asked me to get the laundry basket from her bedroom. I found myself in her room thinking, "What did I come up here for?" We also have problems remembering long-term activities, such as, everyday tasks, brushing teeth, or taking medication. We can be easily distracted by outdoor noises, such as a bird passing by a window. Our attention would be on the bird, not on what is happening inside the classroom. Also, if asked what 5 + 6 equals, one day we might say it was 11; the next day, we forgot the answer.

We also have problems processing information. It takes us longer to process and understand new information. In order to remember something, we have to go over the material repetitively to retain new information.

Four symptoms of ADD are:
1. Fails to pay attention to details or makes careless mistakes in school work or other activities

2. Does not seem to listen when spoken to directly

3. Has difficulty organizing tasks and activities

4. Often loses things necessary for tasks and activities, such as books, assignments, clothes, etc

Attention Deficit Hyperactivity Disorder (ADHD) is very similar to ADD, only with hyperactivity added to the mixture.

Four symptoms of ADHD are:
1. Very fidgety and squirmy in a sitting situation

2. Has trouble being quiet and talks excessively

3. Has problems sleeping

4. May blurt out an answer before the question has been completed

If you believe you have ADD/ADHD, contact a doctor for testing. If you know you have ADD/ADHD, there are options, such as, medications, therapies, specialists, and coaches to assist you.

I have been on medications, such as Ritalin and Wellbutrin. During my childhood, I was on medication for ADD. I did not see much of a difference between when I was and was not taking it. When I was taking Ritalin, I was very focused in my classes and seemed to remember a lot more information. The only side effect was that I could not sleep. Personally, I think Ritalin usually works best for people with ADHD rather than people with ADD.

Since 9th grade, I have not been on medication for ADD. I realized that I work better without it. The plus side was that I did not have to remember to take the medicine every day. If you are on medication and feel as though it is helping, keep taking it. If you feel it has done little to help with your academics, maybe it is time to review and explore an alternative.

What is Dyslexia?
In the word "dyslexia," 'dys' means 'difficulty' and 'lexia' means 'words.' "Dyslexia is a disorder that affects millions of people all over the world. It is one type of a specific learning disability that affects a person's ability to read." (Kuwana 2000)

Dyslexia can be found in many people who have ADD. I have it, as well. A person with dyslexia often reverses the order of letters and numbers. Instead of the word 'their' I may spell it, 'thier,' or instead of the number 23658, I may say 23856. The reasoning varies in each situation. Another helpful term to know when talking about ADD, is "LD," which stands for Learning Disabled. Schools use this term to identify students with learning differences that are influenced by conditions such as ADD/ADHD and dyslexia.

Causes of ADD:
The causes of ADD/ADHD/dyslexia have been linked to genetics. If your mother or father has one of these disorders, there is a greater chance that you could have one also. In my situation, my birth mother had ADD. Taking drugs or drinking alcohol while pregnant can increase the risk of a child having ADD. These two factors increase the chances of having ADD, but doctors and scientists still do not know all the reasons or causes of ADD.

I acquired ADD from my birth mother. When she was growing up during the 1960's, schools did not know how to handle children who had learning problems. They did not have the ADD knowledge that we have today.

Having ADD does not mean that you are stupid or dumb; a person with ADD just learns differently than everyone else. It may take you a little more time to find an answer to a problem, but at least you can discern the answer. Having ADD is always going to be a challenge, but many people have proven that they are capable of accomplishing *anything*, regardless of a learning disability.

I have heard some great metaphors about what it is like to live with ADD.
Here is one of my favorites:

"Everyone has a big hill to climb in life. While the average person walks up, you have to climb the hill with a big boulder attached to your leg. It may take you longer to get to the top, but you can make it up like everyone else."
(Anonymous friend)

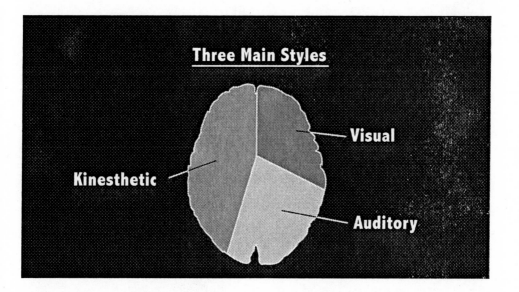

Chapter 3:
Knowing How You Learn

If you are thinking about entering college or are already accepted to one, it is a good idea to know in advance how you perceive information. Review the following three types of learning styles: 1) visual; 2) auditory; and 3) kinesthetic. You will find that you fall into one, two or all three of these categories.

Visual:
If you are a visual learner, you learn best by seeing things. Often, you are very good with reading/writing and remembering pictures. Visual learners should use pictures or words to remember or learn new material. Some students create games in order to study for tests. For example, if you have a vocabulary test for an English class, you could draw symbols for the words. Once you memorize the definition of the word and the symbol together, you will never forget the meaning of the word.

Also, some people remember information by seeing words or examples on a classroom board. If you learn best this way, sit in the first row of the class and keep your eyes locked on the board. When it comes time to repeat the information or take a test, you will be able to remember what you saw and know the information.

Auditory:

Auditory learners learn best by hearing the information that is presented to them. Lectures, books-on-tape, and discussion work well for people who learn this way. It may be a good idea to record lectures and re-listen to what was said in the class-room to effectively remember the required information. Another technique is to form a study group with a few people and engage the students in a conversation on the topic that you need to remember. Or you may want to create a song about the subject you have to learn, such as math times tables! This worked well for me in my high school math classes, even though for me, auditory learning is one of my biggest challenges. Whenever someone communicates to me in words, I often forget what has been said in a matter of minutes. I have experienced that by making good eye contact with the person who is talking; I am better able to remember key words, such as, "paper due on Tuesday."

Kinesthetic:

For people who learn best kinesthetically, it is optimum to actually physically do what you are learning. Computers are a great way for kinesthetic learners to learn. Anything that is hands-on and requires an interaction with the information is a useful way to learn.

In my experiences, I found that visual and kinesthetic approaches work best for me. I have discovered that I learn best through a hands-on experience by connecting the visual part to the hands-on part. I can absorb the information faster and remember it more easily.

By knowing your personal learning style, you will absorb information faster and retain it more effectively; this will truly help you in college and in your career. If you do not know how you learn, there are many tests available online or at your high school. Ask your high school guidance counselor or staff to administer the test to help identify the way you learn best.

I have used my kinesthetic learning throughout my college years to remember and learn information that was presented to me. For example, in one of my design classes, the whole class worked in a computer lab. Each student had his/her own computer. My professor explained how to operate a computer program and the class followed along, step by step. Seeing how something worked in the program and doing it at the same time helped me understand everything that I needed to know in the class.

In my astronomy class, I had to study ten stars and point them out to the professor in the night sky. At first, I thought there would be no way I could remember ten stars. After some thought, I came up with a visual system. I drew pictures of the constellations, memorizing the names of the constellations and the star position in each constellation. When viewing the constellations outdoors, I found it easier to find the them and then to point out the stars.

If I was not aware of the way I learn, I believe I could not have earned the grades that I now have in college.

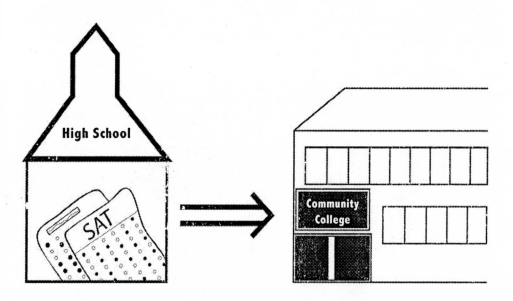

Chapter 4: High School and Community College

High school can be either a positive experience or a negative one. Transitioning from high school to college is scary for everyone, but it can be especially difficult for students with ADD. In high school, there is a lot of help available to you in the classroom. By being in a special ed class, you usually have two teachers who have experience working with students who have ADD. It seems like in high school, your hand is held for you. Teachers are reminding you about assignments and tests, color coding your homework, and making homework guides for you.

Let's face it; you could easily get through high school just by showing up to class and doing minimal work. This is very true for students with ADD who do not care about their education. Most high schools focus on the gifted students who are intellectually, athletically or artistically talented. They do not seem to change or improve their special education programs or go beyond the bare minimum state requirements. There are some special schools dedicated to teaching learning disabled students and know how to help them. Some schools are expensive because of extensive services, but I think they would be worth it.

When I was in high school, I did not care about tests, homework, or anything related to my classes. All I wanted to do was hang out with friends.

In my senior year, it finally dawned on me that I would have to work hard to get into a college. I had to prove it to myself that I could succeed. I researched taking the Scholastic Aptitude Test (SAT). Because I have ADD, I knew that there would be a lot of work involved in just taking the test itself. Additionally, I always had a hard time concentrating when taking tests. I did not take the SATs because they made me nervous just thinking about the test. Also, I was going to a community college where SAT scores were not a requirement.

Even though I did not take the SATs, it may be a good idea to take the test to see how well you do. It is your choice to submit them in your college application or not. A few of my friends who have ADD took the SATs. They reported that the tests were OK if you have your accommodations, such as: extended time when taking the test, a reader, and a quiet place to take the test with no distractions. Always be sure you get the accommodations that you need; it makes a huge impact on your final scores.

One of my friends in high school who took the SATs said that she did have the accommodations, but she felt rushed. She had a reader who read the test to her aloud. Her reader became impatient with the amount of time taken and tried to hurry her through the exam.

This is a good example of when to personally advocate for yourself. NEVER let anyone rush you through exams, quizzes or anything that you, the student, are given extra time for.

A community college may be an option to consider before heading off to a larger university or college. SAT scores are not required, and it will give you an idea about what to expect from college. You may want to take an "Intro to College" class. I took one in the summer before I started school at my local community college. I found it to be helpful, but repetitive. However, repetition is useful for someone who has ADD to retain information. Taking that class can expose and prepare you for what a college class is like, including a course workload.

Visit a local community college to ask questions. Find out which major or majors might interest you. Community colleges do have advantages and disadvantages. The advantages of a community college are usually the following: small classrooms, a lighter workload than a regular university, a college setting that is closer to home and part of your community, and a more affordable tuition. The disadvantages may be a lack of services for ADD students, the choice of majors are limited, and a potential lack of challenging courses.

At the community college I attended, there was a tutoring center. I was delighted, because I thought that I would be getting the maximum assistance from the school.

I entered a certificate program for web design, but found it was hard to follow and spell the words for the HTML code. To me, it seemed like I needed a new major, but I stuck it out to the best of my abilities. I found the workload to be easy, but the accommodations were poor. During my year at the local community college, I signed up for every service the school offered to help me be successful, such as, untimed tests in a quiet environment, tests-on-tapes, books-on-tape for classes, and tutoring. I requested a reduced workload (which means taking two or three classes and still being considered a full-time student), untimed tests with a reader, and a notetaker. I was given my first test and then told to go to another building to get my testing accommodations, which encompassed a reader, extended time, and a quiet place to take the test.

I was given a test-on-tape, but found it to be too fast. I also had questions about the test. There was no one available to ask for help. When I was done taking the test, the woman overseeing the testing area told me to hand it in to my teacher. I could have gone out to my car in the parking lot and copied the answers out of my book or notes for all they knew or cared. It appeared that there was a lack of supervision of students with learning disabilities when taking tests.

My first time at the tutoring center was to garner assistance for a writing class. Everyone in the class was required to remember vocabulary words and definitions for an upcoming test. I could not pronounce the words, so I went to the tutoring center for help. What I did not know was that the center was supervised by students, not teachers or staff. I met with a student who said he would gladly help me. I explained to him that I could not read my vocabulary words. He gave me an odd look, which I did not enjoy. He said, "What do you mean? What do you need help with?" I was thinking, "HELLO, I need help reading these words; how hard is that to understand!" Instead, I calmly said, " I have a learning disability and I have a difficult time reading; can you please help me?" He seemed to get my point and began to help me. I was there for an hour, trying to read my words with him. He finally lost his patience and said, "We have been working on this awhile; why don't you go try them on your own?"

I left the tutoring center feeling angry. Someone who was supposed to be helping and teaching had given up on me and became impatient, just because it takes me a little longer to understand. When you work with tutors, if at all possible, try to find someone who is able to work well with you.

Sometimes, a drop-in tutoring lab is not the best place for someone with ADD to get assistance, as the staff may be less knowledgeable and there is a designated time allowance with the tutors. If your school does offer one-on-one tutoring, this is probably the best option for you. Because the schedule is flexible, you can meet in a quiet place where it is easier to focus and to have the tutor's complete attention.

Some people may have a more positive community college experience than I did; everyone is different and every college is different. A few things I did like about the community college was that it was close to home. I could sleep in until the last minute and still make it to class on time. I also liked the other students who were in my classes. They lived close by, so we could arrange study buddies, if necessary.

Overall, it is a good idea to check out your local community college to see if that is an available option. I am glad I started at a community college because I was able to see what college was like. It gave me the determination to move on to a bigger and better school.

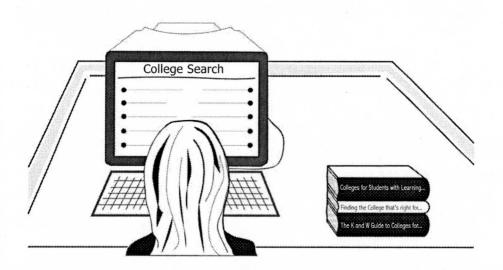

Chapter 5:
Finding the Right College

Finding the right college for you can be a huge challenge, especially if you have a learning disability. I recommend doing an online search first for colleges with support services for ADD students. For example, when I did my first search I typed in a search engine, "colleges with support services for students with ADD." You can also type the broad search word, "colleges." This will provide you with information about all schools and taking the SATs.

If you know what you want to major in, start your search with a subject area to see what type of schools are listed. If you are still in high school, ask your teachers to help you with a search. If you are a community college student, ask the academic advisors questions and keep your eyes open for college fairs in the area.

It is important not to procrastinate in starting the college search process. There are firm application date deadlines. Always know the due date of each piece of information.

After a year of attending and twelve credits later at the community college, I decided it was time for a change and a new challenge. Desperate for a major that fit my goals, I researched colleges that had stronger support and services for students with ADD. I found Rochester Institute of Technology to be my best choice because of the subject majors and the availability of support services.

My parents made various comments, such as, "RIT has 14,000 students! Classes will be huge!" Do not get discouraged if people inform you that they feel a four-year college is a waste of your time. Only you can determine if it will be a waste of your time.

While I was searching for another college, I only focused on schools that had disability services for ADD students, not on the majors. When I located schools that had services, I then looked at the majors they offered. In getting started with my search, I asked an academic counselor at the community college if she knew of any colleges that had excellent services for me. She gave me a book with a section on colleges that offer support services. It is very helpful to do some book research at a library or bookstore.

Books I Recommend:

Colleges for Students with Learning Disabilities or ADD, 7th Edition
Author: Petersons
Publisher: Thompson and Petersons, 2003
(Has very good information about schools.)

The K and W Guide to Colleges for Students with Learning
Disabilities or ADD, 7th Edition
Authors: Marybeth Kravets, MA and Imy F. Wax, MS
Publisher: Princeton Review Publishing L.L.C, 2003
(Great information about what is required for colleges,
lists phone numbers for departments and services.)

Finding the College That's Right for You
Author: John Palladino, Ed. D.
Publisher: Mcgraw-Hill, 2004
(Lists graduation rates, tuition, history of school, requirements,
and services that the school provides for ADD students.)

I compiled a list of colleges; I then turned my attention to the college web sites. I did a detailed search on each college that I was interested in. At this point in your search, it is a good idea to start writing a list of questions to ask the schools and their support service departments.

General questions to ask the school:

1. How many students attend the school?

2. What is the average class size?

These are important questions to ask. With fewer students, professors have more time to give the extra attention you may need, including outside of a class. In a smaller university, there is a better opportunity to know teachers and other students. Having staff and faculty know who you are is very important if you want to get the most help possible.

3. What percentage of your students get jobs after graduation?

4. What percentage of your students with disabilities get jobs after graduation?

5. What is the cost of tuition and how do I qualify for financial aid?

There are a few scholarships for ADD students; you just have to find them. For example, RIT offers the "Bennett Scholarship" which is only for learning-disabled students. As an author, I started my own scholarship for students with learning disabilities. Some of the profits from this book are contributing to that scholarship.

Research on financial aid suggests that 95% of aid is available through the school in which you are enrolled. It is dependent upon your or your parents' income. If you are having difficulties receiving financial aid, student loans are always an option. Check with the college's financial aid department to find the necessary information and forms, and ask them how they can help you.

Questions to ask about support services:

1. What types of services do you offer, and what do I qualify for?

2. Are there any fees for the services provided?

3. What type of documentation do you need in order for me to qualify?

4. How long has the school been working with ADD students?

Some of these questions cannot be answered by a web site. It is a good idea to call the college yourself (**DO NOT** let your parents call for you) and ask them to send you information about the school's courses, services, and other information.

By calling the school yourself, you are learning more about how to get information and you are also showing a personal interest in the school. Some colleges document calls and take them into account during the admissions' process. For example, the staff may write down, "Student called to ask for information about our college." If your parents call for you, they might make a negative comment in your record and note it during the application process. This will show the school that the parents are interested in the school and not the student.

This is especially important for students with ADD, as you may be used to having your parents and school do everything for you. College is the time when you **must** start doing things for yourself (if you don't already).

Once you look over all of the information you requested and you are interested in a particular college, plan a visit to the school to see what campus life is like. During my search to transfer to a new school, I primarily looked at Alfred State College and Rochester Institute of Technology, although I did apply to other colleges in different geographic areas to see if I would be accepted.

I wanted to major in a program that had a design and printing aspect. For Alfred State, I chose to look at Graphic Design. At RIT, I looked primarily into the printing college. I already knew some things about college life at RIT, because I had a few high school friends that attended school there. They all seemed to like it, but they did not know anything about RIT's services for ADD students. My dad and I took a trip to visit Alfred State and RIT.

Our first stop was Alfred State, in Alfred, New York. I called them ahead of time to make an appointment with the Student Support Department. When we arrived on the campus, we walked around to see how large it was. It was very small and looked like a peaceful and private place. However, I was not very impressed with the environment of their support office; it was small, quiet and dark.

My dad and I met with the director of the student support department and asked her many questions about Alfred's services. I compared their services with the services I had at my local community college. They offered untimed tests in a quiet area and notetakers. I felt their services were not strong, but I did like the small campus size and location. My dad was impressed with the services, but he was thinking the same thing I was-that I needed a school with a stronger set of services.

We then drove to RIT in Rochester, New York. Again, I called ahead to schedule an appointment with a staff member who worked in student support services at RIT, the Academic Support Center. Just walking into the center impressed me. There were many staff members walking around; it was busy and full of life. The Support Center representative talked about what services they offered, such as a notetaker, books on tape/CD, untimed tests with a reader, and a scribe if needed.

She also talked about a Notice of Accommodations letter (NOA), a letter that the Academic Support Center gives you to hand to professors during your first week of classes. The letter gives information in detail about the student's accommodations and the professor's responsibilities as required by the Americans with Disability Act (ADA) of 1973. The professors can read what services the student receives, but it does not list the type of disability the student has. It also helps if the student does not talk to the professor directly about his/her disability or the services that are received. This makes the letter more confidential for the students.

The representative also talked about Learning Support Services (LSS), a "check-in service." LSS is fee-based and consists of a meeting held one, two, or three times a week for a half hour to review homework, tests, and upcoming assignments in all of the student's classes. In these meetings, the student receives help to keep track of all classwork and assistance in remembering important aspects of academic responsibilities. LSS would also talk to the student's professors about how they were doing in the class and if there were any problems. The services sounded excellent and exactly what I was looking for.

After both college meetings, I returned home and applied to both schools. I also talked to my mom about the conversations that my dad and I had with the support departments. I told my parents that I strongly felt as though RIT was the best place for me. My dad was still concerned about the size of the campus. Because it was so big, he thought I would get lost. I was also concerned about that, but I knew deep down inside I could handle it. I was accepted to both schools, which was a huge accomplishment for me. I chose RIT because of its extensive services and the subject majors that I was interested in.

Application Process Advice:
A few items you should know about applying to college. It is a good idea to apply to many schools to see which schools accept your application. If you do not get into your first-choice school, you will still have other college opportunities.

1. When filling out your application to the Admissions Office, **NEVER SUBMIT ANY LEARNING DISABILITY INFORMATION TO ADMISSIONS.**

2. In order to get support services, you must fill out a separate application and send it to the support department, not Admissions. This is when (and where) you send the documentation of your disability.

3. This is your college life; do not allow mom and dad do all of the dirty work for you. You should be in control of the whole process; this is all about you.

Some documents you may want to send to support services are:

1. A current Individual Education Plan (IEP) letter from high school

2. Any documents from a medical doctor stating that you have ADD/ADHD

3. Psychological documents such as an IQ test, brain studies or current IQ tests from the high school

Always make multiple copies of these documents; you never know when you will need to submit them.

While I was waiting to see if I was accepted to any of the colleges I applied to, I decided to take a trip by myself to my first choice, RIT. I planned a four-day visit to see what it was really like to go to school there. I stayed in the dorms and walked around the campus. I talked to faculty, students, and staff. It was a fun trip, but four days did not seem to be long enough. I planned a second trip to focus on meetings with the support department and to talk about accommodations. You should feel good about taking time to become comfortable with a college.

Visiting a college is very important and it takes longer than a day to see and ask everything. Take the extra time you need to really see how the campus feels and works. You may want to contact a student who has ADD and is receiving accommodations from the school to show you around. All colleges offer some type of services for ADD students.

While visiting the college of your choice, there is an opportunity to see college activities that may be of interest. There are many clubs, organizations, sororities, fraternities, and other activities available for students to join. Find something that is right for you and that you will enjoy.

Once you have completed the long application process and are satisfied with your choices, then comes the waiting part. Good Luck!

Transfer Students:

If you are transferring from one college to another, contact your college about transcripts to be sent to the new college. Also, contact your high school about transferring your high school transcripts to the colleges of your choice. Sending high school transcripts may not be necessary if you have taken sufficient classes at a community college.

Transferring to another college can be very positive. It is a new college environment, with new people, and hopefully with majors that suit you better. There is also an opportunity to compare classes, services, and other activities with your current and past experiences.

During your college search, friends may tell you about colleges they are looking at, as well. You may consider looking at colleges together with your friends, so that the process does not seem as difficult. It is important to also take note that some of you may be thinking, "Hey, I'll just apply to whatever college my friends apply to and go from there." It is true that you might get into a college using this method, but try to remain independent on your college search to focus on your own needs. Friends can be around forever, but going to college with them or even living with them in a college dorm may be more difficult than you think.

After visiting the colleges that you are interested in, you may feel that you are not into the whole college experience. This is OK; at least you have taken an interest in the process and may have seen other parts of the state or country. As I stated before, "College may not be for everyone." This is true among students with learning disabilities and other students who do not have learning disabilities.

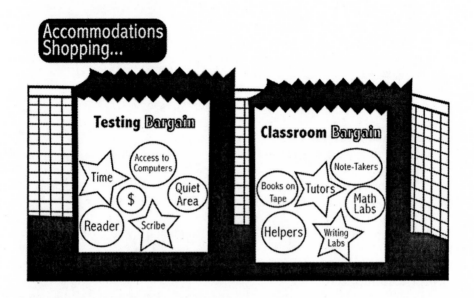

Chapter 6:
Bargaining to Get the Best

At RIT, I received a Notice of Accommodations (NOA) letter and signed up for a notetaker, books on tape, extended time, and computer accessibility for tests. However, I needed a service that was not covered under the ADA and was not mandated by law. I created my own personal accommodation and asked my professors to calculate my grade from a paper that I would write, rather than taking a test for the class. I tend to panic over tests. For example, I will know the answer in my mind, but panic during the test and pick the wrong answer, even though I know the right answer. Sometimes I will write the correct answer to the wrong questions. This can be very frustrating...

My additional accommodation content that I created was in the form of a letter from the Academic Support Center stating that such a service is appropriate to address the differences based on my learning disability. Such a service is not legally required, but allowing me to write a paper would enable me to more accurately demonstrate my education from the course.

I initially spent time speaking to my professors to make sure they agreed to the new accommodation. Most professors have been willing to work with me; others have been a little hesitant about allowing me to write papers in place of taking a class exam. If I find they are not comfortable with me writing a paper instead of taking a test, I usually drop that class and find another professor who is teaching a required class. If only one professor is teaching a required class, I always try to do extra credit in the class to raise my letter grade. I have found that if you ask many questions in a class, it demonstrates that you are trying to learn what you can.

Here are examples of what I received according to my NOA at RIT:

Classroom Accommodations:

"Christina will be using notetaking services for academic course work. The coordination of services will be done through the Academic Accommodations office. She will also be using textbooks on tape. Therefore, advance notice of required readings would enable the Academic Accommodations office to provide tapes in a timely manner. Christina may need additional time to complete assignments and projects. If the instructor agrees, the amount of time should be determined when the assignment is first given."

Testing Accommodations:

"When exams/quizzes are expected to be completed on the same day, the student is entitled to have time and a half for all exams and quizzes with access to a reader. Exams and quizzes may need to take place in a shared testing room in the Academic Support Center. With advance notice by the student, the Academic Accommodations office will be able to accommodate this request."

Other aids that a college may offer are a drop-in writing lab or a math lab. In the Academic Support Center's writing lab at RIT, you can take your papers to have them checked for grammar, spelling, or to have someone read them over to hear how it sounds.

The Lab is filled with experienced staff. They occasionally know the professor who is teaching your class. If they know the professor, they can sometimes tell how you will be graded on your paper. This can be helpful to you for writing papers for a particular professor. You can learn the grading style or paper style of that professor's expectation.

At RIT, TRiO SSS (Student Support Services) provides a useful one-on-one peer tutoring for individual classes. There are a few colleges that have this service. I think it is a great service to look for in a college. The staff at TRiO is always willing to help students. REMEMBER - you have to fill out an application in order to get services.

All colleges are required to provide testing accommodations. When I take a test at RIT, the Academic Support Center provides someone to read the questions out loud. I tell the reader/scribe the answer, and he or she writes the answer down for me. I have found that if I write down an answer to a question, I tend to put it in the wrong place on the test, as I stated before. If I have a scribe write down the answers for me,

I know all my answers are getting proper credit. For essay questions on a test, I will type the answer on a computer and use the spell/grammar check to get my essay to a college level of writing.

Always ask people for help when you need it. Ask your professor. Visit support services. Talk to classmates. Talk about what you need to help yourself figure it out! It will not help you to sit there and give up.

You are in charge of your college degree. You should be able to advocate for yourself. If you are not getting the services you need, tell someone. Explain the situation to the college's director of special services and he or she should be able to assist you.

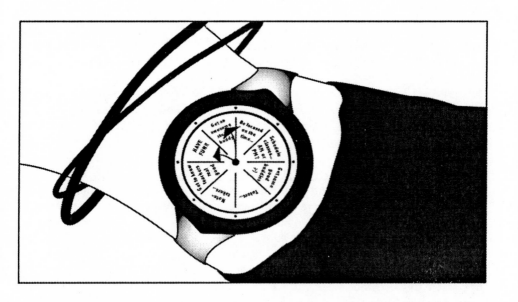

Chapter 7:
The First Year and Other Stories

During my first year at RIT, I found myself a bit scared and confused. I did not know anyone. I had to do everything on my own, although being on my own made me more independent and more capable of doing things by myself.

I do not mean to come across as a mother parental unit shaking her finger at you, but Mom and Dad are not going to be with you at school telling you when to study or go to bed. You, the student, have to come up with a schedule of time management in order to get your work done. Many students can run into distractions in their first year of college. It is important not to let the distractions interfere with your goals.

If you do find yourself being distracted or needing help, locate either a student counseling center to support your needs or ask your college advisor to point you in the right direction. But only YOU, the student, can make this happen.

During the first week of classes, I stopped by the Student Support Center to be sure I was getting the services I needed. By confirming that I would be receiving my services on time for classes, I did not waste my energy worrying about it, as I made sure that problems would not occur during my classes.

I registered for three classes. My first class had 30 students and seemed huge to me, as it contrasted with the average community college class of 8 to 10 students. I took note of the professor's syllabus, which delineated the assignment due dates.

I thought it would be preferable to sit in the middle of the lecture class so I could get a good view of the notes on the board. I saw my notetaker* in the class; he was writing everything down that was on the board. I felt relieved because I could focus totally on listening to the professor.

Over the course of a few lectures, I noticed I was daydreaming a lot. Even when I looked at the notes that my notetaker had written, I realized I did not remember some topics or sections the professor talked about. I decided it would be more beneficial for me to sit in the front row. Sitting up front in the classroom helped me take in the information more effectively.

* It is also important to point out that just because you have a notetaker for your class or classes, this does not mean you are excused from missing a class. Do not rely on your notetaker to do all of your work for you in your classes. He/she may miss some important information that was said in the class. Also, this is your class; you should be listening to what is being said.

At RIT, I noticed that there were a lot of tests in my classes and there was no way out of taking them. My first test was for Digital Image Capture, a very technical class. I studied like crazy because I knew I had to work harder than anyone else in the class just to get a passing grade on the test. I did use my extra time accommodations, but I chose not to take my test in a different classroom. I took it with everyone else to see how I would do. I was not nervous as I usually am in a large classroom taking a test with many students.

However, I found the questions very hard to read without having someone there to explain them to me. I got an F. I studied diligently the night before the test and felt like all the facts and information had leaked out of my head overnight. I decided to talk to my professor about possibly retaking it or doing extra-credit work.

I explained to my professor that I did not test well because of my disability and that I did study and understood the material. He allowed me to do extra credit for the class. He could see that I was trying very hard to understand everything in the class. After taking that class, I have applied the same technique to all of my classes in which I have to take tests.

Sometimes, I will tell the professor in my own words what I have read from the textbook. That way, he or she will see that I really am studying. Do not give up if you studied hard for a test or assignment. There is usually an agreement or an alternative assignment to help you get a better grade in the class. Most instructors want you to be successful.

As I started to get used to RIT's classes and accommodations, things seemed to be running well for me. Although, I noticed that my degree requirements that I signed up for kept changing. I also noticed that I would have to take difficult math classes, such as economics and technical math. In technical math, I learned college-level algebra and trigonometry. This seemed to be overwhelming for me, since I only had a second-grade math level.

I talked to my advisor about my concern with the math and what my other course options were. He said, "There really isn't an alternative to the required courses in your degree."

After careful thought, I knew that I had to do something that was realistic for me to earn my degree. I really loved being a Graphic Media student, but felt I would not be able to learn math at a college level.

I talked with my support check-in staff member. She suggested that I ask the College of Applied Sciences and Technology's Center for Multidisciplinary Studies office about finding a degree that would benefit me.

After speaking with an advisor from the Multidisciplinary Studies office, I decided to switch to an Associates degree with a concentration in Graphic Media. I felt as though this degree would best benefit me, since I have a learning disability. Here was a way to keep my major and also take other interesting classes instead of taking only upper-level classes, such as college math. This was a good balance for me.

In this particular degree program, I was able to choose concentration classes for my major in Graphic Media and select some lower-level classes, such as math classes, that would be easier to understand.

The least strenuous math class that RIT offered was an Intro to Algebra, which was a better fit for me than taking economics or technical math.

My first Math class was a terrifying experience. Initially, we opened the book to the first chapter that contained formulas and funny-looking symbols, none of which I had ever seen before. Leaping from a 2nd grade math level to taking math courses at a prestigious engineering college was not easy. After my first class, I introduced myself to the professor. I explained my disability to him and expressed my concern for keeping up in the class. It turned out that my professor had the same disability as I have. He said, "I have ADD as well, so I know what it is like." To meet a professor who has a disability like mine made all the difference in the world. He was very helpful to me throughout the quarter.

One of the resources I used to master the math was an individual tutor from TRiO. I used my tutor for help with homework assignments. I worked with my professor after class time doing math problems on the board to improve my understanding. Over the course of ten weeks, I started to comprehend what I was learning by doing it over and over again. I received a B (grade) in that class and an A in the Algebra II class. In retrospect, my first college math class was a scary experience, but it all worked out in the end.

In retrospect, my first quarter at RIT was a tough one. I ended up earning primarily C's in all of my other classes. I did very well during my second quarter at RIT. I think I did better my second quarter because I knew my services; I was familiar with the campus, and I sat in the front row in every class. I also managed my time for studying effectively.

Throughout my years at RIT, I have met many professors who have been great to work with and others at the other end of the spectrum who have been difficult. A strong factor for success is to have a good relationship with your teachers. It makes your classes and coursework much easier.

As I mentioned previously, "You, the student have to come up with a time-management plan to get things done." This does not mean you have to become a 24/7, studying student. There will be times when you have to say, **"I CAN'T DO THIS RIGHT NOW; I'M GOING OUT!"** Going out and having fun can be a positive activity that takes your mind off this intense craziness, such as studying for a test or writing a very long paper that you would rather not write. Take a little time off from the task at hand and enjoy yourself with friends or watch a movie. Set a limit for a small break, as it is important to get back to the task.

Another point to think about is whether night or day classes work best for you. There are pros and cons to both types of classes. I personally have taken both and prefer day classes over night. Night classes can be very long. At RIT, they can go from 6pm to 10pm. There are class breaks, but to me, it seems like a very long night.

A student with ADD/ADHD may not want to take such long night classes, because it may be hard to focus for such a long period of time. Try taking the shortest class-time offered, which is held many times during a week. The shorter the classes are, the longer you can focus on the material.

There are positive sides to night classes. Many older students tend to take them, as they work during the day. From my point of view, a night class seems more serious. I believe that I learn more in a night class than if I take a class during the day. Day classes are usually filled with students your own age (which can be beneficial) and you can make friends. Sometimes students do not take day classes seriously. This can potentially distract you or make you not want to learn.

If there is a group project due in your day class, some students tend to slack off the assignment. If you are in a night class filled with mature students, they tend to be more productive and reliable.

Also, if you are a morning person and like to get up and eat breakfast, early classes might be best for you. If you are more of an "I get up at noon" type of person, after-noon classes may work best for you. It is important to realize that some of the required courses may not be available during the times you would prefer. This is when being flexible holds you in good standing.

When signing up for classes, try not to schedule them back-to-back. By having class-es scattered out during the week, there will be time for meals, friends, studying, and sleeping. Also, during final exam week, having three final exams back-to-back will make you have to study very diligently.

During my third year at RIT, I was doing very well in my classes. My grade point aver-age (GPA) was higher than my classmates, which made me feel great. This particular year, I was preparing to start a co-op that I had earned. RIT is well known for its co-op program. In this program, students have the chance to work in the industry that they are majoring in. It provides student experience in the field that they are studying and gives them a vested interest. It is also beneficial to have it listed on your resume.

As I am a printing major, I interviewed with a small printing company in Rochester, NY. I accepted the six-month job and started working immediately. I was nervous that I could not keep up with the job that I was assigned. In the printing industry, you have to remember a great deal of information. Co-workers often came to ask me certain questions. Sometimes, I would panic and forget information. But over a period of time, I became acclimated and was able to answer correctly.

While on co-op, I was concerned about the work pace and my disability. Some people with learning disabilities tell their employer about their disability. I chose to not tell my manager about my disability. I have told previous managers about my disability, who then reacted with a lack of understanding. Some people do not understand what it is like to have ADD. That is OK. While working at the printing company, I realized that some of my math skills were a little below average. For example, I had to print out im-ages on a printer and trim them down to size using an electronic cutter. Before I could trim down the image I had to figure out the measurements to cut the correct amount off of the image. This became very frustrating. I could not figure out how to measure the numbers on the ruler.

Instead of giving up or asking someone else to cut down the images for me, I turned to RIT, once again, for help. I went to TRiO and asked for a cutting tutor, someone who was good at math. They located a graphic design student who had a large amount of measuring experience. I met with her twice a week on how to measure image space and to figure out the amount of paper that needed to be trimmed off of an image.

Over the next few weeks, I started to understand the process. By taking the extra time out of my day to learn something that I needed to know, it showed me that I was able to do just about anything.

Having a co-op opportunity turned out to be an excellent tool for me. By taking a co-op, I learned new things and worked hands-on with the equipment that I would use in my career. It also combined information that I learned in previous classes that I did not understand at the time. I believe a hands on, co-op experience would work well with a student with ADD.

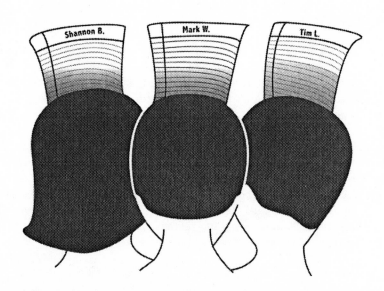

Chapter 8:
Other Students' Stories

I interviewed a few other students who have learning disabilities and have succeeded in other academic environments. They talked about what it was like for them to enter a college. I have spoken highly of RIT, because I found it to be the best choice for me. Find a college that will work for you. There are many universities and colleges that may have the same services as RIT. Find out the information about the schools you are interested in.

Tim Laemmermann:

When I was in 2nd grade, I realized that I had difficulty in reading and writing. I do not have ADD, but I do have a learning disability. My school provided me with an Individual Education Plan (IEP) that gave me extra time on tests in an alternative setting and the use of a computer. My high school met my needs for successful learning very well; I never ran into any problems.

In searching for a college, I chose to attend SUNY Brockport, as it was a small school and had a program I was interested in. The first day I set foot on the Brockport campus, I was extremely scared and did not know what to expect. I found everyone there to be very friendly and supportive. The student support services are great, but to be honest, I did not use them because the professors were very understanding and accommodating. The only time I used the service was when I needed to use a computer for a test; otherwise, I remained in the classroom.

I learned quickly that I worried needlessly. I had no idea what the workload would be like or how tests would differ from high school. The main point I learned is that success is all based on time management; if you can manage your time well, you are golden.

Mark Greenberg:

My name is Mark Greenberg; this is my story. I have always attended a private school, from elementary through high school in Georgia to my college days in Rochester, NY. During my elementary school days, I was never labeled with a learning disability. I remember in 1st grade when I was pulled out of a class occasionally to be tested. Honestly, I never knew what the test was for and I do not remember if I ever knew the results. As far as I was concerned, the tests were just another part of being a 1st grader.

I believe the evidence of some type of learning disability appeared when my school administered the Iowa Tests. I remember feeling anxious about the tests and never liking them. Every year that I took the tests, the same results would be that I was at the bottom of my class. However, when my final report card came at the end of the school year, I was in the top percentage of my class. I remember my mother and teachers telling me that the tests meant nothing; we were taking them so the school could keep its accreditation.

Like most private elementary schools, mine also offered a middle school, or junior high. Students who stayed until the 5th grade would typically continue through the 6th grade and eventually graduate after completing the 8th grade. However, I decided to leave my elementary/middle school after the 7th grade. At that time, my high school offered an 8th grade. My decision to change schools was primarily because I was tired of my parents complaining about the elementary school. The transition to the high school setting was fairly easy. It was at this time I actually found out that I have a learning disability, or so I thought.

I remember going to Emory University for testing and then returning a couple of weeks later for the test results. The woman who did the testing began by explaining to me and my parents what the tests were and what they were supposed to show.

After fifteen minutes of an explanation of the testing and what the results meant, my father interjected, "So what is he?" At this time, the lady looked at him with a somewhat confused look on her face and said, "We don't know, he doesn't fit into any of the categories."

Despite the test results being unclear, Emory University wrote a formal statement that I had a learning disability. I was granted extended time for my tests through my high school's, Student Success Program. (The program was designed for students who had a learning disability.)

I was a good student; I believe I averaged a B during high school. It was during this time that I realized that while I could read at the appropriate grade levels, I was unable to keep up with the reading. It would take me a long time to read for classes,

45

consequently, I would not have time for other homework.

I decided that to be somewhat prepared for classes, I would do what homework I could and let the rest fall into place. This usually meant that I did not read for classes. I would skim parts of chapters or, if certain pages were mentioned in class, I would read those pages. When it came to reading the whole book, that is where I drew the line.

There were times, like in most high school students' experience, when I did not want to do my homework. I remember my high school summer reading when I had my mother read a chapter and then I would read a chapter, as I found it too difficult to sit and read the book by myself. There was another time in 11th grade when a fellow student and I would sit after school and do reading together for my Anatomy and Physiology class. This help finally came after I had failed a few tests and was in danger of failing the course altogether.

While in my senior year in high school, I found out what my learning disability was. The year was half completed; I was being tested for updated college documentation.

This time, I met with a psychologist who told me that he had to repeat the 1st grade because he had a difficult time learning to read. It felt comforting to know that the person performing the test had some understanding of how my mind was working. I was diagnosed with a slight case of Attention Deficit Disorder, as well as a small case of Dyslexia. The psychologist suggested trying some medication, but I did not want to.

As far as college was concerned, I thought that I would not be going to a college, or at least a four-year college right away. My grades were decent, but my SAT scores suffered from my LD. I am probably the only person to ever get his money back from a Kaplan SAT preparation class. I remember running excitedly around the school when, after taking the ACT test, I found out that my ACT score was the same as a four digit score on the SATs.

I applied to two schools and was surprised that I was accepted to both. I chose Rochester Institute of Technology, because the school is technical and has more of a hands-on style that suits me best. RIT also appealed to me because of the school's majors and its reputation as a quality school that focuses on graduates' success. I wanted to be involved with computers, business, some engineering, and at the same time, have a liberal arts education. I decided that majoring in the MIS (Management Information Systems) program would fit that bill.

Looking back, college was a huge transition for me. I had decided to stop taking Ritalin; I cannot say why. My parents, who both have PhD's, went to school near their home in Brooklyn, NY. I was the first in my family to live away at college. I do not think I need to say that there is a weather difference between Atlanta, Ga. and Rochester, NY. My first year in Rochester was livable. For me, my GPA was reasonable for someone with a learning disability and for someone who had picked up his whole life and moved. The teachers were helpful to me, and the staff at the Academic Support Center has always been there to assist.

My strategy to be successful in college was to work hard. I enjoyed working on group projects, because I could then extrapolate on my teammates' ideas and show the teacher that I knew what I was talking about. I learned quickly that grades do not make a person. For that reason, I started to care more about learning the information than regurgitating the lesson back to my professors on a test.

I can ramble on about my college experience, but that is not why you are reading this book. I was asked to tell my story and then give advice, so here it is:

1. You, the student, need to make the decision about what school you attend and what you major in. If your parents make these decisions for you, you have the potential to be miserable. Keep in mind that there are going to be financial constraints. Do not think that because your mom and/or dad went to a particular school that you must go to that school, as well.

Deciding on a major and where to go to school is a tough decision. What I did, and it worked for me, I suggest that you lock yourself in your room for a day or two and write down a list of likes and dislikes of an academic environment and the schools you are interested in. Find out what is important to you and then pinpoint a school that matches those requirements.

2. I would consider going to a community college for a year. It will give you an idea of what college is like. And you can envision what strategies you may need to accommodate your LD.

3. If you have a college and a major in mind, go and shadow a student in your field of interest at that college. See what his or her day is like, so you can see how to accommodate to your study habits.

4. You are going to get frustrated. In fact, everyone in college at some time or another gets frustrated. Because you have an LD, you are going to be even more frustrated. My suggestion is to get involved in an activity that does not require you to write class notes or take tests. Join an on-campus group that attracts your interests. Go to the gym and work out that frustration.

Shannon Baker:

My name is Shannon Baker. Ever since I was diagnosed with an LD, my family has supported me 200%. Without them and the other support I had throughout my educational career, I would not be where I am today. I was first diagnosed in 3rd grade with a Language Processing Problem, which means that I have trouble understanding the spoken word. I need to see what is being taught as well as hear it. I am a visual learner. My services included: extended time on tests at a separate location, the use of a calculator, the use of a word processor and spellchecker, and a question reader, in some instances.

I started my college search earlier than most students. I have an older brother, so when he started looking at schools, I did too. While in high school, my guidance counselor predicted that I would not be admitted anywhere except for Monroe Community College. That statement hurt my feelings. I looked around at Rochester area colleges and researched other schools. I knew that I did not want to go to a four-year school, as I did not know what subject area I wanted to focus on. I applied to three, two-year colleges: Monroe Community College (MCC), Finger Lakes Community College (FLCC), and Genesee Community College (GCC).

Before I applied to these colleges, I met with the school's academic advisor to see what each school had to offer. I fell in love with FLCC. The small campus was a comfortable size for me. When I toured the school, the class sizes were what I was used to...small. I was not going to be just a number in a classroom. When I walked through the doors my first day at FLCC, I was not nervous. I figured that everyone was in the same situation, a new school, new faces, and new teachers.

My two years at FLCC were awesome. If it was a four-year institution, I would have stayed there all four years. The attention that was given to me and the student-teacher relationships that developed are unforgettable.

I attended FLCC for 2.5 years. I transferred to St. John Fisher College. Fisher is a great school, but I should have researched a little more when transferring. Many of the services the admissions counselor said would be available to me, were not. I had to fight long and hard to get what I needed.

Fisher was not a good match for me. As an example, when I took a test, the proctor either would not show up or he or she would fall asleep during the exam. I graduated in May 2003 with a degree in Communications/Journalism and a concentration in General Business.

After months of searching for a job, I decided to go back to school and work towards a Master's Degree. I am currently attending Nazareth College and working towards my Master's in education. At FLCC and St. John Fisher College, I used my accommodations to the fullest. At Nazareth, I have not needed to use them, as I do not have any exams. All of my work is group-based; this learning strategy is beneficial to me.

Here is an example of a support technique that I used: before every class, I handed out a typed letter that I wrote for my professors. It served to inform them about my disability and my strengths. Here is an example of my letter:

"My name is Shannon Baker. I would like to tell you a little bit about myself. I have been coded as having a learning disability. My disability involves a language-processing problem. I am writing to help you better understand my learning style. My strengths are that I am very well organized, a hard worker and motivated. My motivation is the desire to succeed.

My weaknesses are processing information that are spoken out loud. I need to see the words written down. It is also very difficult for me to read and to understand what I am reading. I also need assignments written down on the board. I would like you to be aware of my learning style. In order to compensate for my disability, I need permission to have a separate location for tests, extra time on tests, a calculator, answers written in a booklet, questions read out loud, and a word bank.

My strengths have worked well for me in the past. Also, the assistance from a support person has helped me to achieve my goals. If you have any questions, feel free to ask me. I have a good understanding about my disability and I know what is needed to succeed. Thank you for your time.

Sincerely,
Shannon Baker"

Chapter 9:
Surviving the Long Haul

Going to college may take an extended time to complete a degree. It has taken me six years to achieve two degrees and two certificates from RIT. It is OK if it takes longer than four years to complete your degree. It takes some people more time than others to finish their education. There is nothing to be ashamed of or angry about. I was often asked by my friends, "So why is it taking you so long to finish school?" As I mentioned before, some people do not understand. I tell them that I am taking my time with my education and that the "real world" can wait.

Many parents are often concerned when a son or daughter may not finish in the standard four years. It is important to identify your own skills' pace. College is not a race to see who finishes "on time." While you are in school, you will be expected to take exams or quizzes. Here are some tips for test preparation studying:

1. Take notes in all of your classes, even if you have a notetaker. He or she may inadvertently miss something important in class.

2. Try to study in a quiet location, such as the library or a lab. Do not sit in your dorm room with the TV on, or instant message your friends on the computer or have a CD player on. These distractions will not help you study!

3. Make sure your study area is comfortable, but not so comfortable you fall asleep. Coffee or a soda can be a helpful stimulant for long periods of studying.

4. Figure out what time of day is the best time for you to study. For me, night is always the best time to study. I can focus more on the topic and think clearer.

5. Take breaks! You know you need them. By taking a break you can sometimes come up with an answer or thought about something that is important to remember.

6. Locate study help if you need it. There are often available labs or create a study group with your class. By working as a team, you will tend to remember more information and become more motivated to learn.

7. Try not to procrastinate your studying time. If you have a test on a Monday morning, plan to study over the weekend. Over the weekend means Saturday and Sunday, not dedicating study time to Sunday at 11pm. Study a little bit each day; you will remember more.

8. Create an agenda to manage your day with the activities you have to do.

9. After studying, I always treated myself to something special, such as a movie, ice cream, or a computer game. Taking the time to relax after a long spell of studying always makes me feel better.

The extra years that I have put into my education were well worth the wait. I believe that the longer you are in college, the better. Staying removed from the "real world" does have its benefits. You can sleep in often (unless you have an 8:00am class) and seeing your friends every day is always a plus.

As Mark Greenberg stated in Chapter 9, "You are going to get frustrated." It is important that over the span of years at college you do not wear yourself out. Use your free time to enjoy the experience. Go out, go to the movies, go to a party, go to the gym, and look back on your college life and say, "Yeah, I had fun."

While you are enjoying your college life with friends and studying hard, it is nice to call mom and dad once in awhile to let them know all is going well. Tell them about your grades or talk about the teachers you are dealing with. They will be interested in hearing about the experiences you are facing. I know some of you are starting to say, "Yeah, right," but think about it. Many parents, relatives, friends, or guardians may be helping you pay for college or have helped during your high school years. Let them know how you are doing in school from time to time. They will appreciate hearing from you.

If you have a problem with your accommodations, classes or professors, never give up.

Ask whomever you can to get the problem resolved as quickly as possible. Remember, you are paying for your education; you have the right to receive the support you are entitled to.

If there is something that has helped me in college, it would be pizza, ice cream, beer (but not too much), friends, music, and my own determination to succeed. It is not how smart you are in the end, it is how determined or how driven you are to get there.

Chapter 10: Conclusion

In, *College for Me,* you have read about my journey from elementary school (where I found out that I had a learning disability) to college, where I have succeeded, despite my disability and others' doubts. I hope that hearing my story has shown you that even though there is negativity surrounding a learning disability, high academic and career achievements are possible. If this book has one goal, it is to encourage you, inspire you, and support your dreams. I believe that everyone has the ability to succeed in life, whether or not you have a learning disability.

In today's society, education is the most important step towards that success. At times, the education is difficult and may take you longer to achieve. As you will face more frustrations than the "average" student, you must believe in yourself and know you can accomplish anything.

I have always wanted to help others like myself to achieve their academic goals. Even though this book may not provide the success that you desire, it can be used as a tool to get there.

I hope this book has answered many of your questions about getting accepted to, attending, and succeeding in college. It may seem like you are the only one who is having these difficulties, but always remember, you are not alone. You have the right to get the best education and career you desire.

Good luck and best wishes,
Christina Bryce

-Carolyn **Bryce**-

A Mother's Point of View

This is my mother's experience caring for and supporting me with Attention Deficit Disorder:

The first time I saw Christina, she was a few weeks old. She was born in San Diego, California on May 31, 1981. My husband, Jerry, and I went to California to visit our family, which included Christina's biological mother, Cathy. She asked us to be her Godparents. We agreed to be Christina's Godparents.

She was an adorable six-week-old baby, a little small for her age, but normal in every other way. Her mother was sixteen years old and not always around. Christina was being raised by my in-laws, with lots of love.

One year later, we went to visit San Diego again, and Christina was 13 months old. I noticed that she was not a very friendly toddler and never seemed to make eye contact with anyone. At the time, I thought she did not know us very well.

A few months later, the whole family moved East from San Diego and we began to see Christina more frequently. I thought she was a cold, unfriendly child, with little eye contact towards people.

My mother-in-law asked us to take Christina into our home, as she was getting older. We agreed, stipulating that adoption would provide stability in her life and Christina would know us as her parents. Her mother signed the papers and we had a "Happy Adoption Party." She was two years old when her adoption became official.

The first few months that Christina was with us, she clung to my daughter Becki, who was ten years old. Initially, Christina did not want anything to do with me, but over time, she did warm up. She was not a friendly child. She usually sat on the sofa and sucked her thumb.

I always felt something was not "connecting" in her. While talking with her and watching her, you could see that her mind went from point "A" to point "B" and stopped. There was not a complete follow through; I was sure something was wrong.

Christina's helpful mother,
Carolyn Bryce

A youthful, and very happy,
Christina Bryce

Christina attended nursery school for two years, as did other children her age. She spent two years in kindergarten because of "immaturity." Her teachers always praised her because she was a "good girl" ALL of the time.

Christina started speech therapy in kindergarten and had the same speech therapist for years. She learned to speak in a "Big Girl Voice" because she was timid, shy, and soft-spoken. I still felt something was not "right" and mentioned it to a psychologist whom I knew. The psychologist sent us to a specialist in Princeton, NJ. He ordered a BEAM study. We finally had a diagnosis. There was a right mid-temporal lobe dysfunction and neuropathy, resulting in dyslexia and dysgraphia, as well as many other problems. He prescribed several medications. The first drug, Ritalin, helped her concentrate, but Christina could not sleep or eat. We tried different medications, but none of them seemed right for her.

I knew of a school in Princeton, NJ for children with dyslexia, but it was very expensive and a long drive from our home. A friend of my son's attended the school, so I called his mother to get more information. Fortunately for us, she was an educational consultant and therapist in New Hope, PA. She is the one of the best people who has come into Christina's life.

The consultant/therapist did a great deal of testing. She found that the best way for Christina to learn was through the Orton-Gillingham Method, an older and seldom-used way of learning. Most special ed teachers have never heard of it today. In this method, one touches and feels the letters, like tracing them in the sand and feeling how an E feels and sounds. It would form a new pathway through the brain, so that her thinking could map linearly, A-B-C-D.

Christina was 10 years old at the time and had a short span of using this method, as it would only work until a child is 12 years old. She would then be too old to remap the brain in that way.

The educational therapist worked with me, so I knew what to say at parent-teacher conferences. Because the local schools in our area cater only to above-average, intelligent, college-bound students, we were at a disadvantage.

To save money, Christina's school tried to "mainstream" as many special ed students as possible. I refused to let them do that with Christina. She needed a lot of one-on-one attention. Mainstreaming meant being in a classroom with thirty-five other students with one aide, who was not always present. Christina would never fit well into those classes.

In 5th grade, she was tested by a school psychologist who said Christina would never have more than a 5th grade reading level and a 2nd grade math level. In 6th grade, her male teacher, who could not cope with the rowdy boys in the class, would send her to the auditorium by herself to do her work. It was quiet and she could concentrate, but there was no one to help her with the one-on-one learning that was crucial to Christina's success.

In high school, teachers said that Christina would **NEVER** go to college and was only capable of having a minimum-wage job. She would have to live with us the rest of her life, as she would not be able to support herself. Through Christina's school years, it was a struggle to work with the public school system, as they had little time for anyone who was not gifted.

Christina was gifted in her own way—she had the desire to learn and the drive within her to get a job done. I would love to take her college degree to the high school and show it to all those who said it could not be done. She has and will continue to amaze us with her wonderful desire to succeed.

Carolyn J. Bryce

Comparing Colleges Notes

I designed this section to help a student (like yourself) record information that you need to remember. It can also help you make a decision on which school(s) you like the most by comparing them.

Finding the school that YOU like is the most important thing to remember. Good Luck.

:Notes:

Name of College:_____

Major(s) of interest:_____

_____

_____

**What type of academic schedule is the school on?
Quarters (11 weeks) or Semester? (15 weeks)**

Quarter Pros/Cons:

_____

_____

_____

_____

Semester Pros/Cons:

_____

_____

_____

_____

School Positives: (What do you like)

_____

_____

_____

_____

School Negatives: (What don't you like)

_____

_____

_____

_____

Costs:
(Tuition, disability services)

_____

_____

_____

_____

What types of aid do I qualify for:
(Scholarships, school grants)

_____

_____

_____

_____

Disabilities services offered:

_____

_____

_____

Documents required for admissions:

_____

_____

_____

Extracurricular activities:
(Sports, clubs, fraternities, sororities)

_____

_____

_____

_____

_____

Other Comments:

_____

_____

_____

_____

_____

_____

_____

_____

_____

_____

_____

_____

_____

_____

_____

_____

_____

_____

_____

_____

_____

_____

_____

_____

_____

_____

_____

_____

_____

_____

Name of College:_____

Major(s) of interest:_____

_____

_____

What type of academic schedule is the school on?
Quarters (11 weeks) or Semester? (15 weeks)

Quarter Pros/Cons:

_____

_____

_____

_____

Semester Pros/Cons:

_____

_____

_____

_____

School Positives: (What do you like)

_____

_____

_____

_____

School Negatives: (What don't you like)

_____

_____

_____

_____

Costs:
(Tuition, disability services)

_____

_____

_____

_____

What types of aid do I qualify for:
(Scholarships, school grants)

_____

_____

_____

_____

Disabilities services offered:

_____

_____

_____

Documents required for admissions:

_____

_____

_____

Extracurricular activities:
(Sports, clubs, fraternities, sororities)

_____

_____

_____

_____

Other Comments:

_____

_____

_____

_____

_____

_____

_____

_____

_____

_____

_____

_____

_____

_____

_____

_____

_____

_____

_____

_____

_____

_____

_____

_____

_____

_____

_____

_____

_____

_____

_____

_____

Name of College:_____

Major(s) of interest:_____

_____

_____

**What type of academic schedule is the school on?
Quarters (11 weeks) or Semester? (15 weeks)**

Quarter Pros/Cons:

_____

_____

_____

_____

Semester Pros/Cons:

_____

_____

_____

_____

School Positives: (What do you like)

_____

_____

_____

_____

School Negatives: (What don't you like)

_____

_____

_____

_____

Costs:
(Tuition, disability services)

_____

_____

_____

_____

What types of aid do I qualify for:
(Scholarships, school grants)

_____

_____

_____

_____

Disabilities services offered:

_____

_____

_____

Documents required for admissions:

_____

_____

_____

Extracurricular activities:
(Sports, clubs, fraternities, sororities)

_____

_____

_____

_____

Other Comments:

Name of College:_____

Major(s) of interest:_____

_____

_____

What type of academic schedule is the school on?
Quarter: (11 weeks of classes) or Semester? (15 weeks)

Quarter Pros/Cons:

_____

_____

_____

_____

Semester Pros/Cons:

_____

_____

_____

_____

School Positives: (What do you like)

_____

_____

_____

_____

School Negatives: (What don't you like)

_____

_____

_____

_____

Costs:
(Tuition, disability services)

_____

_____

_____

_____

What types of aid do I qualify for:
(Scholarships, school grants)

_____

_____

_____

_____

Disabilities services offered:

_____

_____

_____

Documents required for admissions:

_____

_____

_____

_____

Extracurricular activities:
(Sports, clubs, fraternities, sororities)

_____

_____

_____

_____

Other Comments:

Resources

↳ Lloyd, Pamela. Disability Services Agreement (NOA). Rochester, NY: 2004-2005.

↳ Natural Pure Health. Attention Deficit Disorder - ADD – ADHD and What You Can do About it. 16 April, 2002 http://www.naturalypure.com/AttentionDeficitDisorder.htm. 10 August 2005

↳ Psych Central. Attention Deficit Disorder. 2005. 16 April 2005 http://psychcentral.com/disorders/sx1.htm. 10 August 2005

↳ University of Washington. Kuwana, Ellen Dyslexia. http://faculty.washington. edu/chudler/dyslexia.html . 10 August 2005